under the yellow lights

vee beato

under the yellow lights

poetry

under the yellow lights copyright ©2019 by Vee Beato.
Book Cover ©2019 by Vee Beato.
All rights reserved.
No part of this book may be used or reproduced in any manner whatsoever without written permissions except in the case of reprints in the context of reviews.

ISBN: 9781790896424
Imprint: Independently published

*for the lion-hearted
and the soft*

contents

wall of gratitude……………...…………………..……..7

affirmation jar……………...………………………....58

mirror mantra……………………………...…………...84

under the yellow lights

i'm keeping this wall of gratitude
i will fill it with my thoughts
about how happy i am
until all the sadness
won't have space to come in

wall of gratitude

vee beato

one day
you will wake up
with a tray of honey toast
and a cup full of loose-leaf tea
with lemon slices on your bed
you will see the morning sun
just waking out the window
you will see the green trees
rustling softly, carrying a cool and crisp breeze
you will be glad that you wake up
you will be glad that you are alive

good morning

under the yellow lights

you look happier

the best compliment

vee beato

and one day you will be happy
that you stayed alive long enough
to meet someone that is good
at loving people like you

under the yellow lights

you should never forget
that even when you're not looking
the light is always there

vee beato

it's the small things
wearing yellow shirt
and water with freshly squeezed juice
people that just seemed to exert positive vibes
and sleepovers
rekindling friendships
and forehead kisses, cheek kisses,
nose kisses, kisses in general
these things are so small
but they mean a lot to me
it's not the amount of things
'big or small' that should matter
but the way you appreciate it
choose the things that don't make you
slide it aside for a little while
choose the things that make you feel
you are somewhere else
and not somebody else

do the things that let you be who you are

                    under the yellow lights

yellow painted walls
and sunflowers in white vase
string of candid polaroid photographs
and flickering fairy lights on shelf
chamomile tea
and handpicked berries on tray
scented candles
and new books on bed

gold moment

vee beato

there's always a hug
to tuck you up
when you start
to feel sad

hug all your friends

under the yellow lights

i'm slowly healing
and learning how to be brave
just like the stars
and its light
that carries on even after death

vee beato

in a field of sunflowers
you will still try to find
the yellows that look
sunniest for you

under the yellow lights

learning to love yourself
will always feel like
riding a bus
on a weekday afternoon
there's a little bit of nostalgia
and pure coming home

you'll find your true self by learning to love it first

vee beato

one day
you will find
the right way
of saying *you are beautiful*
and it will matter again

under the yellow lights

you are ordinary to everyone
until you meet the one
then you are magnificent

vee beato

let's just stargaze
all night long

under the yellow lights

i'm lying under the sun
it's cold and quiet and blue
i'll let the sea swallow me now
so that i'll be there with you
but i'm here, washed up
a million miles away from you

vee beato

how beautiful it is
that the universe is made
just to be seen by our eyes

under the yellow lights

i want you to feel safe around me
i want your lips to kiss my collarbones
i want you to bury your face
into the curve of my neck for me to hear you breathe
i just want to be the reason why you breathe

that's all that matters

vee beato

maybe the purpose
is to make people
stay longer

under the yellow lights

i always look up at
the sky full of stars
every night
only to help me see
how the world and people
are bigger and worthier
than their sadness

vee beato

when people leave
you'll think in the long run
that you have nothing left
you're wrong
there will always be
the morning sun
your soft bed
cute pet
clean slate
and your tougher self

under the yellow lights

after the rain
the earth will
still smell of love

petrichor

vee beato

and it is his softness
that promise to make them closer
to each other
and over time
eventually fall in love

find soft

under the yellow lights

the hardest thing to destroy
is the fear that causes you
to hold on into something
when you should let go

vee beato

being hopeful starts
with realizing that today
someone is getting ask for a marriage
someone heard the news
about having their first baby
someone just gotten their dream job
better days are coming
it could be today or tomorrow
don't let anything
take you away from being strong
your life is now
and now could be your life

today could be your greatest day

under the yellow lights

all i want
is a warm relationship
that lights up
my existence

vee beato

so much potential
this human race
so much

under the yellow lights

hearing that sleepy
"i love you, self"
before going to bed
is always my favorite moment

things i don't forget to tell myself

vee beato

and i'll take some time
to be thankful that
i had days full of you

under the yellow lights

you will romanticize the way
his lips form into a smile
in the lull of the morning
and realize that beautiful people
just happen

vee beato

i am headed
somewhere warm

under the yellow lights

there will be a time
that you will come home
to a place where
every single thing you see
will tell you to stay

choose to be alive

vee beato

boys
and sun-clotted hairs
running over roofs
and constant rediscovery
of who we are

kings of summer

under the yellow lights

thank people
for existing

vee beato

on a starry night
amongst the constellations
where you wrote my name
you'll always find me there

when i'm gone

under the yellow lights

i won't close this
little corner in my heart
for the people who hurt me

vee beato

if you're ready to go
just kiss me hard
and whisper to me
a song

goodbye

under the yellow lights

and it's your eyes
that broaden these horizons
telling me to look
because there's
a big world out there

vee beato

he imagined loving him
would feel like
falling in love with sunshine
dazzling, a little painful
and always lovely
because the flowers bloom with him

                        under the yellow lights

some days are
for falling in love
with myself

vee beato

keep close to me
you stay cozy

under the yellow lights

i always say distance is a curse
but maybe it's a cure
someday i'll go somewhere far
where it doesn't hurt no more

vee beato

falling in love
with yourself
is having a heart
that is proud of itself

under the yellow lights

and if happy is a place
i hope they have a space
for me and you

vee beato

at some point
we're always unmindful
that happiness is reflexive
as a little kid is
for the colors we see once
we open our eyes for the first time in the morning
and breakfasts
for the literatures on the shelves
and the people who find
joy in reading them
for the sunny days
and clean swimming pools
for the rainy days
and warm blankets
we always forget that
once we see these things we smile
we always forget
about that beautiful feeling

always appreciate the moments that you are happy

under the yellow lights

i have witnessed you
and for me
that's enough

vee beato

when you look at people
with big smiles
you see how small
your problems are

under the yellow lights

happiness is an act
of endless forgiveness
from ourselves

vee beato

even when we're
too shy to admit
we knew

skinny love

under the yellow lights

i really like it when strangers ask me

have we met in a different world before?

vee beato

if you turn your back
to being happy
you're automatically
turning your back on yourself

please don't do that

under the yellow lights

the best thing about
loving the little things
about yourself is that
you will never
ran out of space
to keep them

they will fit everywhere

vee beato

affirmation helps you accept
what you are becoming
and it makes it easier
tell yourself the things
you need to hear
and if it's difficult
write it down
put it in a jar
then recreate yourself
wildly
boldly
and continually
until you like what you see

affirmation jar

under the yellow lights

loving yourself
is the greatest
rebellion

vee beato

even the littlest flower
attracts butterflies still

no matter how small you are
you will always attract those who believe in you

under the yellow lights

you deserve bundles of flower
and cups of coffee
you deserve notes left on your cupboard
and books as a gift
you deserve kisses on the cheek
and hugs at night
you deserve things that remind you
that you are loved

vee beato

today i'm a stardust
but tomorrow
i could be
the universe

under the yellow lights

the kindest thing
you can do
for someone
is to love them
even when they're
still learning how to

vee beato

it's hard to fight wars alone
maybe they aren't there for you yet
because they are fighting their own wars too
but i promise you the only truth i know
you are loved

so loved

under the yellow lights

and if you feel like
you are not enough
i'm here to remind you
that you are

vee beato

you're thinking about quieting
your heart down
but please
have the courage to believe
that someone someday
is going to be soft and kind with it

under the yellow lights

you can offer
her sunflowers
or you can be
her own sunflower

vee beato

you can be made of stones
and still has sweet exteriors

under the yellow lights

and you will wax and wane
from new to full
and back to new again

moon witch

vee beato

you are not a star
for lost people
to find themselves

under the yellow lights

you will be
the kind of perfect
to your right someone

they would never want you to change

vee beato

there's always a sun
to remind you
to follow your fire

under the yellow lights

after all these
i became vulnerable
but ironically
i reassure you
nothing's going to
hurt me anymore

vee beato

you look like
all the bright places

under the yellow lights

you are primarily
responsible for the
falling and rising
of the ocean tides
inside your body

sun and moon

vee beato

and if they give you rain
i promise to give you sunshine
so you'll see the rainbow

hope

under the yellow lights

be the sun to those
who need to see the
morning flowers

make someone's heart happy

vee beato

i don't fear
getting comfortable
with being alone
to be strong
is to be good at it

under the yellow lights

i am enough
for my self

i always have been

vee beato

you've been with yourself
all your life but
why is it so hard for you to remember
who you are every time

under the yellow lights

and if you
don't deserve
the whole universe
you deserve more

vee beato

one day
all the feelings
you thought you'd forgotten will come
but remember you are an ocean
let them sail
let them swim
until you're ready to let them drown

                    under the yellow lights

shine brighter
than all the yellows

vee beato

i will look at this mirror
and i will see what is more than
the face who is always staring back at me
always asking where to find happiness
i'm not going to look for happiness any longer
i'm going to work towards it
i will pave my own path because
no one will do that for me
not to chase happiness
but to meet it

mirror mantra

under the yellow lights

yesterday morning
i couldn't get up my bed
couldn't read
couldn't write
couldn't listen to songs
without having a heavy heart
and couldn't figure out the point
today, i woke up early
dressed up
and right now, i'm dancing to a tune
and i'm making myself breakfast
i figured that there is no point
you just got to live what you feel

ride it out whatever it is and live in the moment

vee beato

it's okay to lose
someone again
as long as
it's not yourself

under the yellow lights

to make them listen
that is the goal

vee beato

these nights will come
the low moods
the tired feelings
the dark sides emerging
but they're nothing
because i will still breathe
and i will still love life

it's okay not to be okay

under the yellow lights

there's light
even in the
places you hate

vee beato

you can never figure out
what your life is about
but it should not stop you
from exploring yourself
throughout the journey
you'll find out that
there are so many
interesting things
about yourself
if you look for them
hard enough

under the yellow lights

you are as sad
as you want to be

vee beato

i know the feeling
of not loving
someone back
that's why
i stay out of it

under the yellow lights

and you're unable to love a person
the way you'd want
because another one
has already taken the most of you
you have loved already
and too much
nothing
isn't it too strong of a feeling

vee beato

i honestly don't know
why i crave for your voice
it makes me feel empty
in a way that it hurts so much
but i guess that's what i need
to remind myself that it's over

under the yellow lights

he smelled of sea salt
because his tears
always belonged to oceans

boys can be emotional too

vee beato

she is fire
she warms
then she destroys

girls are strong

under the yellow lights

tell me how am i
supposed to pack my bags
when you're the home
i can be human with?

vee beato

it's hard to love
when you don't know
how to love anything
so you have start with one place
yourself

self-love

under the yellow lights

i don't love you anymore

that's all he wrote

vee beato

let's make moments
like we're in a song

under the yellow lights

we always fight
each day and night
to make it out
of our heads alive

sometimes we don't realize how strong we are

vee beato

you have to learn
for yourself that
setting free
all your illusions
that something
could have been
any different is needed
in order for you
to carry on

under the yellow lights

i've realized that
i'm always trying
to look for myself
in other people
plainly thinking
that maybe
i'd be as beautiful
as they are

i need to get rid of this insecurity

vee beato

be honest
if you tell yourself
that you love yourself
then do it
it shouldn't have to cost a lot
browse second-hand bookshops
grab your morning coffee
smile at the barista
take pictures of your food
change your perspective about the world
it's not yet full of happy people
and there will always be a room for you
this time you're not doing it
just for yourself because
if you mean it
it would also mean to somebody else

things i need to do today

                  under the yellow lights

face the world
holding your own hands

vee beato

get bored
with your past

it's over

under the yellow lights

the only love
i need right now
is a love that listens

a love from myself

vee beato

if only
keeping you close
makes you
love me most

under the yellow lights

get excited about little things
about wearing the same
fresh laundered outfit
going to the theatre
about friday brunches alone
about calling him before he go to work
and before he sleeps at night
about the new songs and movies
he shows you
about getting a new hair color
about anything that even
slightly makes you giggle
because as you mature
excitement fades
and keenness gets mistaken for
idiocy and silliness
hence, don't let the ideas which
people think little of and fail to appreciate
stop you from being yourself

note to self

vee beato

and if you think
my softness
makes me vulnerable
wait until I make it far

under the yellow lights

i want to go
on a place
where nothing but
my happiness exists
where all that
i have to lose
is myself

vee beato

maybe you didn't like the sun
and you got tired of burning your skin
maybe you didn't like the smell of salt in the air
and your feet on the sand
maybe lukewarm is no good for you
but i am summer, love
and you came a little early for the rain

under the yellow lights

your skin isn't like
the stem of sunflower
don't cut it

vee beato

there is no map
for you to seek
all the bright places
in yourself but
you will walk
there soon

under the yellow lights

you look at other people
and you look at yourself
and it scares you
it scares you that you know
what would you do for people
it scares you that you don't know
what would you do for yourself

list of things my mom told me i should do while waiting for someone:

1. it's easy to sulk and feel isolated when you don't have someone in your life but it's okay. enjoy your life alone. learn what you like and dislike. give yourself a hard, firm timeline to stay out of relationships

2. distract yourself. go to the theatre alone. sit inside the coffee shop alone. read books. you don't have to shut yourself into the world. you just have to do the things that make you happy alone because once you are contented, you'll be less likely to jump into a relationship for wrong reasons

3. try traveling alone. be courageous. you'll find traveling alone therapeutic. plus, you'll have a great, interesting story to tell on the first date

4. you know how easy it is to jump into a relationship at the first sign of sparks but don't do it

5. don't use a friend as a crutch to fill the void of any lost relationship

6. you have to understand what you like and what makes you happy in order to find yourself. learn what you love. discover your goals. write down your priorities

8. you need to remember that there's always give and take. make sure that you have a firm understanding of when and where to draw the line. make sure that any relationship moving forward allows you to be yourself and achieve your goal

                          under the yellow lights

now that you let yourself fall in love
the next thing you need to do
is to remember that free-fall
always end in two ways
you get back up again
or you miss your limbs

is this exactly why you're scared

vee beato

i need a calm like sunrise
an existence like sunshine
a hope like sunset

i am a sunflower

under the yellow lights

the only goal i have
in my life right now
is to inspire people
i hope someone someday
will remember me
and tells himself
"i'm glad i didn't give up
because of this person"

make people remember you about the good things you've done

vee beato

breathing good vibes
like air

under the yellow lights

everything i do
is a way to be
loved a little more

aren't we all

vee beato

to like yourself is
to like what you do
and how you do it

under the yellow lights

i don't wish that you were here
i only wish that you are
where you wanted to be

sacrifices we make for love

vee beato

don't spend
the majority of your life
just rolling in the wind
without direction
don't go from
nowhere to nowhere
make it your personal mission
to live a life
you are proud of
something you can bring up
because it is remarkable

under the yellow lights

you'll kill your dreams
with your fears
more than your failures
ever will

vee beato

you can't just mix
honey and poison

cut toxic people out of your life

under the yellow lights

it's okay to fail
and start over again
just remember
how much we want
to catch raindrops
in our cupped palms
even though
we know it will
always slip away

this is how we grow

vee beato

do what you want to do
live the way you want to live
it's not always what you need
that you must do
sometimes you must go
for what you want
you are yourself
before you are anything else

if that can make you happy, go for it

under the yellow lights

healing will only begin
once we accept the fact
that people are meant
to fall into pieces
like the stardust we all are

and we will become stars again

vee beato

sometimes you are
confined to four walls
and that's it
no one is really
bounding you there
but yourself

under the yellow lights

you should take some time to reflect
on how much you've grown over
the last few months
in any way
like having your very first job
or a new one
gaining new interests like
painting and meditating
starting new journals
doing the same habits like
having iced tea or hot espresso
in your favorite coffeehouse
and watching movies in the theatre alone
or just becoming more empathetic towards yourself
you should remind yourself
that growth is always there
and that it doesn't need
to have a huge impact
in your life to hold a value
you are growing in every way
and these moments often lead
to beautiful experiences

vee beato

some people need to
slowly fade away
from my heart

under the yellow lights

we need someone
who makes our morning better

vee beato

you give a little of yourself
to what you spend your energy to

a reminder to only do things that make you happy

under the yellow lights

all this time i thought
i was writing
for the happy ones
but i've been writing
for the sad ones

acknowledgements

without veronica and ananias, my parents, *under the yellow lights* would never have been. thank you so much. they were there to believe me and encourage me throughout my journey in writing this book

mrs. dela cruz, my high school english teacher, my best friend, thank you for all the knowledge you shared and making me realize that language is important

irene were there for me since day one with advices when we go out for a coffee and a movie

joyce, i owe my confidence to you. thank you for being my voice when i couldn't speak

marife, my dear cousin, thank you for listening to my stories and giving me hugs, kisses, and laughters. you truly define happiness

a very loving thank you also to manilyn, christine, jessa, sarah, mary, rizza anne, emily, elaiza, krizza, monique, beverly, marian, jenevie, pauline, sofia, and christiane dave for teaching me what friendship means

diane, jacki, stefan, peter, jigo, and diego, thank you for the courage

and the biggest thank-you of all to my past students, they are great reminder to pursue passion and they bring light to my future

Printed in Great Britain
by Amazon